The River Running Through Him

Kaye Nelson Ratliff

Goose River Press
Waldoboro, Maine

Copyright © 2020 Kaye Nelson Ratliff

All rights reserved. No part of this book may be reproduced in any form without written permission from the publisher, except by a reviewer who may quote brief passages in a review to be printed in a newspaper or magazine.

Library of Congress Card Number: 2020936200

ISBN: 978-1-59713-215-2

First Printing, 2020

Cover photo and author photo by June Witherspoon.

Published by
Goose River Press
3400 Friendship Road
Waldoboro ME 04572
e-mail: gooseriverpress@gmail.com
www.gooseriverpress.com

Dedication

This book is dedicated to my wonderful family, husband Ashe, children Stephen and Ashley, and grandchildren Jacob, Benjamin, Katie, and Eli. They are my inspiration and the loves of my life.

Table of Contents

Leaving Home//1
Lines Written on a Paper Napkin//2
Night Song//3
Storm Coming //4
Little Boys and Turtles//5
Predestination//6
Reflections on "Annie Freeman's Traveling Funeral"//7
Advent//8
Aphasia//9
Autumn Meditation//10
Childhood Remembered//11
I Am Woman//12
Katie's Song//14
Midsummer//15
Oak Island 1971//16
Lovers' Fourth of July//17
Wandering//18
The Calf//19
The Wren//20
The Darning Egg//21
The Man Who Troubles My Dreams//22
Daddy's Song//23
Old Dog//24
Love in a Minor Key//25
When I am Old and in the Nursing Home//26
Zen Dying//27
Traveling 109 on a Winter Evening//28
Traveling 109 on a late Spring Afternoon//29
Traveling 109 on an October Day//31
Pentecost//32
Soul Journey//33
Class Reunion//34

Table of Contents

Moorings//35
Prissy//36
Twilight Longings//37
Solitude//38
En Español//40
Grassy Island//41
Of Cats and Dogs//42
At the Greek Festival//43
The Healing//44
The Angry Stick//45
Happily Ever After//46
Loving Peter Pan//47
Susurrations//48
Graduation//49
I Stopped to Write a Poem//50
Missed Things//51
Morning Walk//52
Parting the Red Sea//53
Resurrection//54
The Need for a Poem//55
The River Running Through Him//56
November Rain//58
Two Haiku//60
A Drive Through Town//61
Reflections on a Vulture in Flight//62
Homecoming//63
Mothers and Daughters//64
Through a Mother's Eyes//65
Union//67
Carolina Christmas//68
A Reflection on Yeats's Poem//69
City Silence//70

The River Running Through Him

Leaving Home

Clayton Sutton doesn't live here anymore.
He never looked back to see who watched
as he closed the door of his boyhood home
just up the block from me.
His family gone,
the girl gone up to Boston,
folks said he'd go to Europe,
spend his fortunes there,
or lose himself in some artistic dream.

But I know he'll sit beside a mountain stream
to listen for the answers to the questions
he once put to himself and me—
sitting in the garden by the wall—
and fling pebbles at the answers.
He'll gather flowers in a meadow
and toss them at the wind
then chop wood for a fire
to build his fantasies in.

1968

Lines Written on a Paper Napkin

Once we shared warm summer days
dining on ham sandwiches,
drinking white wine from paper cups.
You decorated our world with rose petals
and wrote poems to me on paper napkins.

But they are not long,
the mellow days of youthful summer.
Now, out of a smoky past
comes a vision of whirling bodies
dancing to the songs of our love.
You had a look of confidence,
a look that knew
where we would go from there.

Where do they go
the honey days,
the mellow months of summer?
Where is the autumn
of sweet desires and golden dreams,
of plans and promises for the wispy days of spring?
False spring,
you have no roses,
no Rhine wine,
not even daisies for a nuptial chain.
Did you not leave me
even so much as a petal?

1968

Night Song

The night breeze whispers through the window by the bed
joined by a mockingbird's pretenses,
arousing, enchanting my sleep-protected senses
to memories of old love songs
and other mockingbird melodies.
I am startled awake as from a terrible dream

to the tune of my drumming heart
and the cacophony of my reeling mind
blending with the song of the melodious betrayer
outside the window.

I reach for the sleeping form beside me
undisturbed by these night players,
lying still, and warm, and solid,
and edging closer, his arm comes round to hold me.
The breeze dies,
the mockingbird stops his song,
and sleep returns its blanket
to still the night.

1973

Storm Coming

Clouds and treetops
argue the fate of the sky;
with squirrels as audience
and blue jays for critics,
high drama unfolds
at five o'clock.

1980

Little Boys and Turtles

What is it about little boys and turtles?
Little boys can keep up with turtles.
Turtles eat worms and dead flies.
Little boys aspire to.
Turtles love muddy water,
as do little boys.

What is it about little boys and turtles?
They love long, lazy summer afternoons
adrift in sunshine,
crawling through the grass,
each contemplating the nature of the other.

Oh, that little boys grew as slowly as turtles!

2008

Predestination

There are many who chase God
through dark corridors
of mind and heart.
There are many more
who do not chase God
at all.

I do not chase God
because God has chased me
and found me in my hiding place
and told me
"Tag, you're it!"

2008

**Reflections on
"Annie Freeman's Fabulous Traveling Funeral"** *

Come!
Join the traveling funeral!
See life from every side and every place.
See the people as you hurry on your way
to where your ashes will hurl themselves
into the wind.

Come!
Join the funeral procession,
the throngs of faces familiar and faces strange
dancing toward that destiny
each one meets along the way.

Come!
Life is the traveling funeral
winding its way through the streets
of Time and Place,
gathering the mourners
as it goes on parade
from one beginning to the next.

2008

*A novel by Kris Radish

Advent

Come slowly, Christmas.
Last the whole December through,
'til every child has seen Santa's sleigh
coursing through winter's night sky
and every grown-up knows
it is indeed a Wonderful Life
and every church in every town
has put the pageant on
with Mary, Joseph and the Christ Child
center stage.

Come slowly, Christmas.
Sing to us your sleigh bell songs
of snow-bright days and crystal nights
when candle-lit carolers come to call
at houses decked out in twinkling lights
that rival the starlit sky.

Come slowly, Christmas.
Make each December day a joy all its own
as we watch Dickens Carol once again
and assure little Virginia there is a Santa Claus.
Then on that final, special day,
when the floor is a sea of crumpled paper and bows
and the feast is all consumed,
remind us that the Christ Child
whose natal mass we celebrate today
will someday seek our presence at his cross.

December 2009

Aphasia

The winds of time blew through my mind
and scattered all the words around
like so many falling leaves,
and now I cannot find the letters
to say what's in my heart
or tell the story of shared memories.
So tell me of times we've had
and of our days now past,
so I can know you loved me then
the way I love you now;
for who knows what we'll lose
when the wind blows again.

2009

Autumn Meditation

Sitting in my morning place,
looking at the world outside my window,
I see the chickadee perched there
on my favorite maple tree,
waiting for his turn at the feeder near the porch.
Maple tree's auburn leaves are glowing
in October's morning sun
and I stay still, enamored by
the beauty of the scene.

As I watch this gift unwrap before me,
sunlight, bird and maple tree,
I come to realize the gift includes me,
that I am one with all of these.
Your Word, Creator God, spoke life
into the bird, the tree, and me.
Your Spirit, Lord, blew through the tree,
gave song to bird and breath to me,
and blessed us all in your creative scheme.

Bird, now from the feeder filled,
flies off to other glorious scenes.
Sun creeps higher in the sky
spreading light to grace the day
and tree holds tight to radiant leaves
before the wind whips them away,
and I in raptured adoration raise
thanksgiving for the bounty of this day.

2009

Childhood Remembered

For Pat and John and Reg

The night breeze whispers across my skin
like the flutter of a fairy's wings.
Traffic sings softly on rain wet streets
through windows open to the sweetness of the night
accented by the songs of chirping crickets
and the misty glow of streetlights.

The awakening of my evening senses
gently brings memories of other street nights
chasing each other and playing games
while grownups creaked the front porch swings
and the scent of petunias drifted on the air.

Too quickly they left, those summer days
and times of carefree childhood games.
But perhaps some night you'll sit and feel
the stirrings of an evening breeze
and remember the times we had back then,
and remembering, perhaps you'll smile.

2009

I Am Woman
For the Opening of the Anson Women's Center

When you think of me,
how do you think of me?
Do you think of me as wife, as mother,
as daughter, as lover?
I am all these things,
but I am more than these,
so much more than these.
Let me tell you who I am.

To Naomi, I am Ruth:
faithful daughter, sister sojourner,
life companion,
listening for the wisdom you teach me,
the guidance you give me.
To Ruth, I am Naomi:
caring mother, guiding mentor,
knowing teacher,
passing to you the wisdom of women,
redeeming us from danger and sorrow.

I am Helen, whose beauty beguiles men.
I am Athena, whose wisdom defies them.
I am a creator of life and beauty,
a giver of language and of art,
adorning the world with color and song.
I am the softer, gentler side of humanity,
bringing justice without violence,
healing without pain.

I am Woman.
I am the other face of God.

August, 2009

Katie's Song

Eyes the color of gathering storm clouds
or pre-dawn mists
has my Katie.
Hair like kitten silk
and a smile that beguiles like a moonbeam.

Little fairy child
with laughter that sparkles like dewdrops
steals my heart with her Erin charm
and rides me on wild pretended ponies
across heathered meadows of her making.

Daughter of my daughter,
heart of my own heart's heart,
enchant us a little while longer
and let tomorrow wait.

2009

Midsummer

It's the season for Granddaddy Longlegs
and the fourth of July is now another memory.
The fragrance of gardenia and jasmine has faded,
yielding to the brilliance of crepe myrtle in bloom,
and the sun hangs hot and high in the sky.

Watermelons ripen in sandy patches
and sunflowers nod their heads in the afternoon sun
while corn stalks stand tall in defiance
of the withering heat.

Stay with us yet awhile, Summer,
and give us firefly nights
and lazy lemonade days,
to remember with longing
when winter comes
and turns our hearts to icy stone.

July, 2009

Oak Island, 1971

We made our home once by the sea
where we could watch the moon dance on the ink black water
outside our bedroom window.
The wash of waves upon the shore was our lullaby
and cradling in each other's arms our final evening's joy.

We savored the scent of salt in the air
as daily we walked upon the beach
offering our faces to the caress of wind and sun,
and collecting the treasures offered up by the ocean.
Music floated to us from a nearby carousel
lending a lyrical pattern to life that was our magic charm,
and we considered ourselves to be lavishly rich.

And thus it was that moon and tide
wove themselves into the fabric of our days
enchanting us and making us believe
that life and love would always be this way.

2009

Lovers' Fourth of July

Fireworks over,
picnic guests gone home,
we sit alone
while the rain drums softly
on the awning overhead
and Sarah Vaughan sings love songs
just for the two of us.

Firefly and candle flicker
illuminate the rain scented night
as quietly we sit,
in an intimacy only old lovers can know,
sharing this gentle interlude
and wishing the rain would never end.

July 4, 2009

Wandering

When I grow old, I may start to wander.
If I do, please come and find me.
These are the places you should look:

Look for me where the moonbeams
draw a path on dark blue waters,
or in the garden where spiders write
the brief and tangled stories of their lives.

Look for me where kittens tumble,
or where small boys do the same.
Find me in an October meadow
sneezing from the fresh-cut hay,
or on a Carolina mountain
watching the sun creep over the range.

Seek me on the front porch,
rocking in my favorite chair,
on a rainy summer evening
smelling the sweetness of the air.

And the last place you should look for me
is behind the smile that lights my face
when I see you standing there.

2009

The Calf

I want to see a calf run.
    I saw one run once
        driving by a meadow.

He ran as if
    all of life were in the running
        and I laughed at the pure joy of him.

I want to see a calf run.
    I saw one run once
        driving by a meadow.

2010

The Wren

She did it again this year-
that bird, that silly wren-
built her nest in the middle fern
that hangs on my front porch.

Old Black Snake will come soon
for the eggs
and I will need to watch for him
to take him back
to the woods across the way.

When will they learn-
that bird and that snake-
caught in their survival game?
They seem almost human
the way they do over each year
the things that don't work.

2010

The Darning Egg

Alabaster white and porcelain smooth
the darning egg slipped into the sock
where mother's tiny stitches
mended the hole.
Sneaking into the dresser drawer
I held its weight in my hand
and pressed its coolness to my cheek.

Where is it now, I wonder,
recalling the feel of it against my skin.
Perhaps it landed in an antique store
with other of my family treasures
where some other woman finds it there
recalling childhood memories of her own.

Or perhaps it lay in a landfill
with other cast off things
waiting to be unearthed
by some future archeologist
wondering what ancient bird
gave birth to such a wondrous egg
thousands of years ago.

2010

The Man Who Troubles My Dreams

He came again last night—
the man who troubles my dreams.
Perhaps it was the Brando movie—
Stanley howling for his Stella
while the cameras played
on the glistening, rippling muscles.

He came again last night—
the man who troubles my dreams,
the man with no face or name,
the man with no present or past,
the man who howls my name,
calling me to run with the wolves.

2010

Daddy's Song

My Daddy's favorite song was Stardust.
Hearing it, he'd get a wistful look,
and I wondered what he thought about.
I rather think it wasn't mother,
but only Daddy knew.

My Daddy's favorite song was Stardust,
but there were other things he loved:
movies and Broadway shows, and baseball
and everything about New York.
And me. My Daddy really did love me.

At just fifteen, my Daddy ran away from home
and sailed to foreign ports, and saw the world,
and went from one adventure to another,
learning to love the stardust of distant skies.

My Daddy's favorite song was Stardust.
He'd sit in his chair, cigarette smoke curling 'round his head,
 with that faraway look in his hazel eyes,
hearing not just the song, but the romance in his soul
when I played the tune he loved.

My Daddy's favorite song was Stardust,
but now its melody calls out to me.
So it's only fair to tell you, friend,
I'm so much like my Daddy.

2010

Old Dog
For Maggie and Eli

Fall City, Washington
April 29, 2010

Hello, Old Dog.
We've brought another baby home—
a boy this time.
I hope you'll stay around a while,
he'll need a dog, you know.
He'll want to pull your ears and tail
and sit upon your back
as though you were a pony ride.
He'll need a dog to pull him home
should he get near the road,
and run across the lawn to fetch
a stick he'll throw.

Was that a kiss, Old Dog?
I saw you lick his tiny face
and lay down by his crib.
Thanks, Old Dog—
I thought you'd see it my way.

Love in a Minor Key

When I was young
love was a symphony,
big and grand,
booming brass,
sonorous strings
played in a major key.

But now youth is gone,
yet love plays on,
rich and mellow,
saxophone smooth,
a moaning cello—
love in a minor key.

2010

When I Am Old and in the Nursing Home

When I am old and in the nursing home
please do not let me sit in ugly anonymity,
but daily bathe my aging frame,
and put some make-up on my face,
and line my eyes with kohl
so that perhaps someone will look into these eyes
and see the lingering youth within my soul.

2010

Zen Dying
In Memory of GC

Go, gentle spirit
into the Light you tried to show us,
toward the Moon to which you pointed
while we could only see the finger pointing.

Go, gentle spirit
into the great Cloud of Unknowing,
your bowl kept empty on this earth
now filled with the brilliance of eternal sunlight.

Go, gentle spirit
leave your lumbering body behind
enjoy the fulfillment of enlightened mind
and journey on from night to everlasting day.

2010

Traveling 109 on a Winter Evening

The orange-rose glow of the setting sun
spreads its molten flow across the sky
as we ride through the winter evening.
We see it peak through the black lace-work of trees

then burst in glory over empty fields
white splotched from last week's snow.
It holds our gaze so long we almost miss
the graceful silhouettes of deer leaping

across the road, impeding our forward progress.
The river reflects the dying light
as it wanders through the pines.
Wrapped in the blanket of this silent scene

we sit not speaking, afraid we'll break the spell.
Then near the limits of the town
night overtakes the setting sun,
and as we look towards the lights ahead

we see the cold white rising of the moon.

2011

Traveling 109 on a Late Spring Afternoon

Traveling south,
the western sun warms my face
in the air-cooled car.
How well I know this road
 traveled so often
from his hometown to mine
and back again.

This time of year
Queen Anne's Lace fills the ditches
bordering the newly plowed fields.
And there's the barn at Rocky Creek
with its new red coat of paint and green tin roof,
a reborn relic from a farm long since gone.

Only two small towns
sit on this stretch of road
 and one hardly that,
if not for the factory there,
where Hispanic workers now replace
the Laotians who came once
in the migratory ways of humans.

The stretch across the river is the best,
 past all the homes on both sides of the tracks,
 then nothing but miles and miles
of pines and oak and birch,
and the dull satin ribbon of the river,
and the sun blinking brightly
through the windows of the car.

And still I can't decide
which direction I like best—
towards his hometown or mine.

2012

Traveling 109 on an October Day

Here I am again on this familiar stretch of road
that holds memories of other trips
I've made on it, and how it has made me.
I feel the familiar warmth of the sun
shining in the window,
meeting the crisp autumn air
and I feel more alive than on any summer day.

Fields of cotton, Southern snow,
spread themselves against their woodland borders
where the rich greenness of the pines
is overpainted with reds and yellows and orange;
and where there are no pines the sunlight melts
like gold on hardwood trees.

Southern forest, ancient Uwharrie range,
you were home to bear and deer and native people,
long before this road was cut for wagons,
or paved for me to ride.
Ancient river, running through primeval hills,
what is the baptism you baptized me with
that makes me long for home?

2012

Pentecost

Daily I march in plodding obedience
to worn-out creeds and soulless dogma,
desperate to feel the joy of peace
and the freedom of spirit-filled bliss.

Weary of flash-in-the-pan religions
and the either-or that amounts to the same,
I long to feel the wind of the Spirit
blowing through my soul

 and fanning the fire that blisters my tongue
'til it sings the song burning deep in my heart.
I want to feel flesh and sinews on these dry bones,
enlivened by the breath of God.

So I stand on the mountain embracing the wind,
and thrill to the shudder of the earth beneath.
I welcome the scorching heat of the fire
yet still my soul is unfulfilled.

In despair I descend into the depths of silence,
surrendering the longings of my mind and heart.
Then there in the utter stillness I find
the Spirit of the Living God.

2012

Soul Journey

Oh Soul, let's leave this failing flesh
and flee to dance on moors
we never got to roam,
and float on our backs
in that Ionian Sea.
We'll climb Tibetan mountains
as though they were gentle highland hills
and race each other across the Asian steppes.

When we tire of our frolic on this earthly plain,
we'll hitch a ride on Apollo's cart
and feel the warmth of the sun,
 then stop off at Olympus
to give Zeus a piece of our mind,
and tell Hera she should be ashamed.

Then on to the stars where we'll make
faces at that crabby constellation
 because we're Sagittarian born.

 When we've finished this existential frolic,
 we'll soar to the highest of heavens,
and spend the remainder of eternity
resting at the feet of God.

2012

Class Reunion

I saw you standing across the room
talking to your friends.
I wanted to come to you and say hello
but I feared you would not remember me.
I remember you.
 I remember the touch of you,
the scent and taste of you,
the firm, smooth feel of you.
 I only wanted to say that I forgive you;
forgive the selfishness of you,
the cold dismissiveness and cruelty of you,
the painful unlovingness of you.
But I could not have forgiven you
for your not remembering me.

2013

Moorings

There you are, sitting on the dock
fishing pole in hand,
 the sun playing its light
on the dark gold curls of your hair,
and I stop
to savor the look of you there.

Sometimes this is how I love you best—
at a distance, visible but separate,
your own distinct self apart from me—
untethered from the anchor that I am to you.

Isn't this what love is?
A thing that ties us down inside,
then bursts forth,
freeing us from its moorings?
allowing us to drift on its tide?

2013

Prissy
Story of a Beloved Dog

Again today she waits by the road,
but when the time for coming passes,
 she knows the boy will not be home today,
just like all the other days she's waited.
So the old dog walks around the house
and into the woods, settling into a bed of leaves
 near the cave where he'd found her
when she'd whelped her pups,
just by the tree that fell in the storm,
where the boy and girl would walk the pirate plank.
She nestles in the leaves and remembers
how they jumped together in the piles of leaves,
and how they wrestled in the yard
and rolled together in the snow;
how she'd raced downhill with them on their bikes
and waited for them outside the store;
 how she'd walked them safely to the school bus through the woods,
 then meet them in the afternoon.
She remembers and she knows some day
 he'll come and find her here,
and as she dreams and waits,
the light grows dim, as does her life,
for what else is she to do
a dog without her boy.

2013

Twilight Longings

Sitting here in the garden in the gloaming,
I see the fairies dancing,
twinkling in the fading light.

Yes, I know they're fireflies in the twilight,
not fairies in the gloaming;
and yes, I know this blanket 'round my shoulders
is not your embrace,
nor the whisper of the wind
upon my cheek your kiss;

but the coming night beckons
and memory beguiles—
and, God, how I wish they were fairies!

2013

Solitude

There comes a time for solitude-
for sitting alone on the porch or in a park,
 watching the people go by,
 wondering about their lives.
Or listening in the twilight
to sounds of the evening,
feeling the night wash over your skin
and savoring the mingling
of sweet aromas in the air.

There comes a time for remembering
the sweetness of being sixteen
sitting at a drive-in,
car windows open to the summer air
and feeling the stirrings of life
in body and soul.
Or the skin memory of holding your baby
close to your breast,
or the embrace of a lover.

There comes a time for solitude-
for contemplating how to be one
with all things,
like the squirrels chasing along the fence,
or the leaves emerging from their winter's sleep;
or how to crawl into the heart of God
and rest there.

There comes a time for solitude.
So how do I tell
this clanging world around me
that time has come for me?

2013

En Español

The July heat comes off the parking lot in waves,
the only shade the canopy over the gas pumps
where I insert my card preparing to fill my tank.
That's when I hear the salsa music
 throbbing from the pimped out old white Chevy
cruising through the Walmart lot,
 windows down, driver leaning out.

  As he passes I see a handsome light tan Latin face
leering out the window.
 We make eye contact, and he nods
smiling wickedly,
and when I look back at the pump
I have pushed that button that says
"En Español, por favor."

2014

Grassy Island

Up the Pee Dee River lies Grassy Island
the place where sons and fathers go
to celebrate the rites of passing
from boy to man.
They call it Naked Native Island
for there they shed their mothers with their clothes
 becoming brothers to each other
and to wolf and bear.

A canoe comes up the river
bearing a man
shaking the rattles of stone and snake
wearing the charms around his neck
 chanting some ancient chant
and with his coming the wild riot begins.
Ropes swing from trees
carrying boys out over the river
and fires blaze and boys whoop
while grown men sit around the fire
conjuring up the stories
they will pass to their sons.

At dawn, the fire is damped,
the boats are packed,
and men and boys head home
 to mothers' care and the civilization
that binds like the clothes they wear
returning to school on Monday
with secret knowledge in their hearts.

2014

Of Cats and Dogs

Because I have no cats,
I have birds.
Oh, I have a dog,
 and the birds fly from her—
but she isn't interested—
only in squirrels.
The squirrels bark—
not the dog—
the birds sing,
the breeze blows, and I—
I am content.

2014

At The Greek Festival

We come for the souvlaki and the baklava
and step into an ancient marketplace,
welcomed by a bright cacophony
of vendors hawking their wares,
and music from balalaikas and tambourines
playing for gaily clad young dancers
 performing ancient dances.

The air teams with the aroma of baking honey
and roasting lamb
and our eyes are dazzled
by the brilliance of color everywhere.
Then I see the faces,
the same ones I saw on the statues and urns
in the museum across the way;
faces that have escaped the erosion of time
 that claims nearly everything else.
Is that the face that launched a thousand ships,
 the beautiful one
talking to the one so like the god Apollo?
My senses are a time machine,
transporting me across the millennia,
 my mind joyous at making this delirious leap.

Then my companions turn to me to say
that it is time to go,
and reluctantly I cross the threshold
 returning me to ordinary time.

2014

The Healing

Ten lepers get healed that day
and the Preacher tells them "be cool,
 don't go blabbing this all around."
But you know how it is with lepers:
they run to the Temple
to show off their smooth skin,
join the Establishment,
yuck it up with the Levites,
start a support group.

The young Preacher shakes
his head and thinks,
"But there was that one,
that one who came back."
So he hurries on his way,
knowing he hasn't much time to rest,
before the Word gets out.

2015

The Angry Stick

She picks up the stick,
the just right-sized stick,
good for hitting the ground
the trees and the bushes
without breaking.
A good stick for getting out the mad.

But when she uses the stick
the mad gets so big
and heavy and hard
she can't carry it any more.

So how does a girl child say it hurts?

2016

Happily Ever After

Do you ever look back?
On your girlhood dreams, I mean;
the dreams you dreamt in your
pink fluffy room,
full of gingham and lace.
Did Prince Charming ever come
and sweep you off to his castle
to live happily ever after?

Or did reality come instead
 and chase the dreams away?
Did something hurt you so
that you no longer dream?
Or do you plod along,
still in glass slippers,
refusing to look back,
to dream of things that might have been,
the pinks of life fading into the grays of your days.

Then what if life, with all its peccadillos
handed you another chance,
a way to begin to dream again,
would you take the chance?
What's that you say?
I cannot hear you
through the noise that is your life.

2016

Loving Peter Pan

Flying wingless through the night,
fueled by pixie dust and fairies' dreams,
he lights on my window sill and casts
his shadow on my wall, and offers me
 a thimble full of love.

With tales of high adventure he lures me
to a land where Indians haunt the woods
and pirates sail the seas
and lost boys raise the mighty ruckus
'til they fall asleep
and dream of mothers they no longer know.

Time and I move on but he does not;
then comes the day his shadow doesn't linger on the wall,
and a thimble lies empty on the nursery floor,
and memory fades the magic times we shared.

Yet looking from my window in the night,
I see the third star on the right glow bright,
while a familiar cloud shape sails across the moon.
Then I remember how sweet life was
when I loved Peter Pan.

2016

Susurrations
> *Definition: whispering sounds, murmurs*

A meditation on Psalm 62

Our lives are but a breath upon the earth,
whispers from the mouth of God.
He breathes in and we live,
he breathes out and we die.
He declares YahWeH, "I AM,"
and we tremble with fear
for our being.

Yet with susurrations of longing
in the depths of our souls
 we softly cry
"Breathe on me breath of God."

2018

Graduation
Asheville, May 2019

Pomp and Circumstance,
solemnly progressing,
a timeworn ritual
precisely followed.
Four years condensed
to one final hour.

Lofty words
and great expectations,
cheers and tears
and silent prayers applied.
Mortar boards fly
like bats disturbed.
An end that is a beginning.

But the spider weaves silently
in the corner,
oblivious to all designs
but her own.

I Stopped to Write a Poem

I stopped to write a poem this morning,
the one that sang in my head all night
so that sleep could not come easily.

Why do poems do that-
always come in the night-
when there is no pen or paper
or light to shine on them,
so that we chase them round in our brains
to keep them alive until dawn?

Poems are like faeries in that way.
They flit and flutter around in our heads
while we try to catch them with nets of words.
I wonder if this is why
 there are so many Irish poets?

2019

Missed Things

I miss sandwiches on white bread
and lime sherbet.
I miss sidewalk skating
with a skate key on a string around my neck.

I miss cowboy movies on Saturday
at the Carolina Theater
and the aroma of the soda fountain
at the drug store.

I miss rolled-up cuffs on blue jeans
And bobby socks and oxfords
And sock hops at the gym.

I miss Elvis Presley and Marilyn Monroe
who taught us about sex and rock and roll.
I miss convertible rides on springtime nights
and first kisses and drive-ins.

But most of all, I miss
that first stirring of love
awakening the woman inside me
and wondering what comes next.

2019

Morning Walk

Cats huddled in furry piles
await their morning feeding;
spider webs wet with dew
glisten in the rising sun;
and school children at the bus stop
 shrug shoulders against the crisp cool air.

The road and sidewalk are filled
with yesterday's detritus,
while grandfather's beard vine
flows over walls and shrubs and lawns
like spilled milk.

Oh, what a beautiful morning.

September, 2019

Parting the Red Sea

The thrum of the motor sounds like a tribal drum
as he rides the Harley down the river road
covered in a sea of red autumn leaves,
past the church that still has slave galleys
where captive people prayed for a Moses
 to set them free from their bondage.

The leaves part in the wake of the powerful bike
and the rider wonders as he rides through this sea
if he would have been a Hebrew savior
or one of Pharaoh's army.

2019

Resurrection

When the grass dies
or a sparrow falls to the ground,
does God care?
When the butterfly emerges from the chrysalis
And falls prey to the mantis that becomes dinner for the frog,
does God see?

When the mountain born in violent eruption
is worn to sand by the soft and steady wash of water,
and the vast ocean becomes a cloud
that gives its life to nourish the earth,
where is God in this eternal game
of rock-paper-scissors?

Doesn't' everything in creation die
only to be resurrected,
 enduring in another form,
so that nothing in heaven or on earth ever really dies
but lives eternally in cosmic unity
with the One who created it all.

 I wonder then, what and where we'll be
when our resurrection comes.

Lent, 2019

The Need for a Poem

I need, today,
a Mary Oliver poem.

Grief and loss are nibbling away
at the corners of my mind
eating away at the hope
and gladness I have stored there.

So I read of black bears
and black snakes shedding skin
and foxes waxing wise

to try to restore the balance
of life in this world
and the things that I love.

2019

The River Running Through Him

Between Griffin's Low Ground and Ingram's Landing,
the Great Pee Dee arcs north briefly,
giving wide berth to old farms along its banks,
 then heading south through the Carolinas
to join the vastness of the ocean.
It is nourished along its journey
 by the creeks and swamps
  where he has hunted and fished since boyhood,
  like his father and grandfathers,
   becoming, with them, a part of the river's life.

Below the Lumber Landing the river pours over the dam
creating Blewett Falls—built by fearless men
 who drank and fought as hard as they worked,
some staying buried there, interred in the concrete,
human sacrifices for theft of the River's power.

He's seen the river flood once, almost reaching
 the peach orchards near the highway bridge.
The old men told him stories of pushing down
the heads of cattle with poles,
forcing them under the old bridge
when flood waters washed them
from lowland meadows below the falls.
And he's seen it so dry it seems you could walk
from the Lumber Landing across to Grassy Island.

C-130's cruise low above the river,
one crashing there once, in Blewett Falls Lake,
where they say there are catfish as big as a man.
The crew is buried there with the dam builders,
and who knows how many others
share this watery grave.

His children were baptized with the mud of this river,
and it lives forever in their blood.
He fell in love on its banks,
 and it blessed the union
with the gentle sounds of its wash.

He taught his son to be a man on this river,
and grafted the love of it into his soul.
Once father and son put in below the dams
and let the river take them to where it joins the sea,
 completing the initiation of another generation
 into this sacred life.

He's seen where the river begins in Carolina hills,
and where it ends at Carolina shores,
running through his life on its journey,
 as essential to him as the blood in his veins,
anchoring him to this place he calls home.

2019

November Rain

I remember the rain that November
the day the cat died.
His pleading eyes looked at me
as if his god had forsaken him.
A big black Maine Coon,
with leonine features and attitude as well,
we had taken him from people who
didn't want him anymore.

They were the ones who forsook you
I wanted to say. Instead
I loaded him in the car
and took him to the old vet
who was dying, like the cat.
He was as heavy in my arms
as the rain pouring from the heavens
and the god that seemed to be
away from us both.

The rain is not heavy this November day
as I walk my morning path.
It is soft and fine and touches
my face like a kiss
when the wind blows it against me.
The day is soft, too, no cars
passing by, no sounds on the street,
only me wrapped up in my coat
with my umbrella
and the men who always run
and nod as they pass.

I stop to put the paper
on the old woman's porch.
I do not want her to fall trying
to fetch it from the wet walkway
where it has landed.
Besides, I like to look at the raindrops
glistening like crystal
on the long-leaf pine on her lawn.

This path I take is a labyrinth
I walk every day,
a place of contemplation
where my mind is free to wander
and to wonder.
Poems appear here,
as well as prayers and
thoughts of people who need them.
And I meet cats, lots of cats
along the way
that recall the Maine Coon.

Things die in November,
but unlike my cat
I will probably live
 through this rainy day
and perhaps I'll see the sun
 come out tomorrow.
After that,
who knows.

November, 2019

Two Haiku

Kittens

Young kittens tumble
in new-mown dew-wet grasses
tigers in their hearts.

Dandelions

Dandelions grow
though humans do not want them.
Roses fade away.

A Drive-Through Town
In honor of the Ansonia Theater

It's just a drive-through town,
a place to stop if you want to,
but you don't have to;
a place to fill up
with fast food and fuel
before going on your way.

But what if you made a right-hand turn
and meandered through its streets
to see the drama of life
played out on its stage
 by actors who are people
just like you.

What if you stayed to witness
the joys and pains of the players
in this show that you would miss
if you just drive through.

Perhaps there would be
a role in this drama for you.

2019

Reflections on a Vulture in Flight

There's something dead in the woods.
Vultures are circling overhead again today,
the late afternoon sun lighting
the underside of their wings with gold
as they soar as beautifully
 as any eagle in flight.

Scorned by human kind,
they go about their business
of completing the circle
begun by purveyors of death
known by loftier names.

Reviled raptor, do you know
that your presence brings a chill
to living creatures,
while the dead cherish
your cleansing power?

2013

Homecoming

I hear the familiar rattle
of the wooden bed
of his truck,
and smile.
He's home.
His supper simmers on the stove
and the children eagerly watch for him
from the front room window.

He's home.
In the door he comes
asking for his dinner
and greeting me with his kiss.
He smells of the scent of men
who work in the sun
and I gladly drink in the musk of him.

He's home.
And that magic time called normal
begins again.

2009

Mothers and Daughters
for Ashley

As I watch my daughter
watching her daughter,
and delighting in her child's delight,
I think of my own now long-dead mother
whose beautiful face and joyous laughter
graced my childhood days;
and then I see these same soft graces
reflected in my daughter's face.
Recalling the tears I wiped from her eyes
and the feel of stroking her hair in my lap,
remembering her laughter and her flashing green eyes,
I realize that bright eyes and laughter
passed from one mother to another
will go on when I, too, am gone.

August 10, 2009

Through a Mother's Eyes
for Stephen

There stands a man of forty years,
with graying beard and hair,
a preacher in a pulpit in a long black robe,
but this is not what a mother sees.

A mother sees a babe in her arms
snuggled to her breast,
a babe she rocks to sleep
as she dreams of the life that is to be.

A mother sees a toddler of two
following his father into the sea
with no fear of the ocean's might
because he's in his father's hands.

A mother sees a boy of nine
jumping in piles of leaves
and wrestling with his dog;
a boy and dog roaming through woods
searching for adventures.

A mother sees a youth of 16,
engaging in the firsts of cars and dates,
and proms and football games,
anticipating the life that is to be.

A mother sees a young man of 18
going off to school
facing new oceans and new woods,
coming home to find the faithful dog no more.

A mother sees a man in his twenties,
experiencing adulthood's firsts
of marriage and babies and new career,
of moving on to other new oceans
 and other new woods.

Only now can the mother see
the man of forty with graying beard and hair,
the preacher in the pulpit in the long black robe,
going into the oceans and woods of life,
now in his heavenly Father's hands,
living out the life that is and is yet to be.

2009

Union
> *for Ashe*

Rays of morning sun reveal the thread
spun between the car and truck.
 I hesitate to break the silk
linking our two vehicles.
How does the spider know
we're still connected,
even when we're apart?

June 19 2012

Carolina Christmas

It's Christmas time in Carolina.
Snow falls softly in the mountains
and fog rolls inland across the Outer Banks.
The lonely whistle of the Seaboard train
moans its way along the southbound tracks
that slice through tiny Carolina towns.

Horses and cattle munch on fields of frosty grass
that have replaced summer's early morning dew,
and deer abandon the woods in search of acorns
found in neighborhood yards.

It's Christmas time in Carolina.
In the cities, shoppers swarm the malls
where lights and glitter are strewn everywhere
reminding me of department store windows
in my own hometown,
where toys came alive and trains circled round,
and children lined up to sit in Santa's lap
and the downtown streets were criss-crossed
 with colored lights.

It's Christmas time in Carolina
where Church yards still boast the Christ child's birth
and every tree blooms with twinkling lights
and children still act in nativity plays;
where carolers still sing at a neighbor's front door,
and we go to bed on Christmas Eve
with dreams of Peace on Earth forevermore.

Christmas, 2009

A Reflection on Yeats's Poem*

When I am old and grey and full of sleep
there'll be no book to tell that my eyes
had a soft look or of the changing
landscape of my face, but only your

remembrance of my being in this place;
and what will you remember of me then?
That I lit passion in the minds or in
the hearts of men? Will you recall a woman

full of grace and love and brave enough
to fight for causes lost and causes won?
And when I flee to mountains overhead
and hide among the stars, will I care

whether you remember me at all?

2013
* " When You Are Old," by William Butler Yeats

City Silence

Silence is different in the city.
Like a lover it caresses me,
whispering softly, allowing only the
ambient sounds of birdsong
and humming noises of the distant street
to brush against my soul—
protecting me from the bruising noise
 of planes overhead
and the rumble of giant machines.

At night it is the hum
of wheels on wet pavement
and the distant whistle of a passing train,
or a siren racing far away.

It is the silence of imagination
and poems written in my mind.

2011

Kaye Ratliff graduated from the University of North Carolina at Greensboro with a BA in Psychology in 1967, and from the University of North Carolina at Chapel Hill with an MSW in 1986. She worked for Sandhills Center for Mental Health, Mental Retardation and Substance Abuse Services from 1974-2006, beginning in Mental Retardation Services, then as a Licensed Clinical Social Worker after receiving her MSW. She was the Unit Manager in Anson County, supervising the staff as well as providing therapeutic services to adults and children. She retired in 2006, and provided consultant services and clinical supervision until 2015.

Mrs. Ratliff is married to William Ashe Ratliff, and is the mother of two adult children, the Rev. Stephen Ratliff and Ashley Ratliff, and the proud grandmother of Jacob and Benjamin Ratliff and Katie and Eli Haynes. She is an ordained Presbyterian Elder and is active in her community where she has served on many boards. She and her husband reside in Wadesboro, NC.

While at UNC-G, Mrs. Ratliff developed a life-long love of literature and poetry. She belongs to the Anson County Writers Club, and currently serves as its President. She enjoys writing poetry and short stories, often writing stories for her grandchildren. She also enjoys her hobbies of reading and crocheting.